HC

D1189075

NATO

Reg Grant

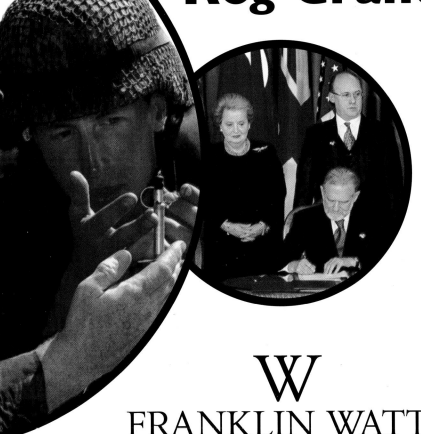

W
FRANKLIN WATTS

This edition 2004
Franklin Watts
96 Leonard Street
London EC2A 4XD

Franklin Watts Australia
45–51 Huntley Street
Alexandria NSW 2015

© Franklin Watts 2001 and 2004

Series Editor: Anderley Moore
Designer: Simon Borrough
Picture Research: Sue Mennell
Franklin Watts would like to thank Chris Bennett,
the editor of NATO Review, for his help and advice
in compiling this book.

A CIP catalogue record for this book is available
from the British Library.

ISBN   0 7496 5694 8
Dewey classification 361.6

Printed in Malaysia

Picture credits:
Cover: NATO br; Popperfoto l (Reuters/Kevin
Capon), r (Reuters/Yannis Behrakis)
Inside: Corbis p. 4 b (Bettmann); Corbis-
Bettmann p. 26 (AFP); Hulton Getty pp. 8
t (MPI/Truman Library), 14 cr, 14 br & bl
(MPI Archives); Magnum Photos p. 12 b
(Philip Jones Griffiths); NATO 5 t;
Popperfoto pp. 11 (Reuters/Viktor
Korotayev), 1 r (Reuters/Jeff Taylor), 2 t
(Reuters/Paolo Cocco), 2/3 b
(Reuters/Yannis Behrakis), 4 t (Reuters),
5 b (AFP/Persson), 7 (Gary Hershorn),
8 b, 9 t, 9 b, 10, 11 t (Reuters/Dswa-
Dasiac), 11 b, 12 tl, 12/13, 13, 14 t, 15 t
(AFP/Alexander Nemenov), 15 b
(AFP/Gennady Tamarin), 16 (Reuters/
Paolo Cocco), 17 (Reuters/Viktor
Korotayev), 18 t (Reuters/Danilo
Krstanovic), 18 b (Reuters/Jeff Taylor), 19
(Reuters/Benoit Doppagne), 20 (EPA/S.
Pikula), 21 t (Reuters/Benoit Doppagne), 21 b
(Reuters/Yannis Behrakis), 22 t (Reuters), 22 b
(Reuters/Yannis Behrakis), 23 t (Reuters/Paul
McErlane), 23 b (Reuters/Petar Kujundzic), 24 t &
b (Reuters/Emil Vas), 25 (Reuters/Chris Helgren), 27
(Reuters), 28 cr & c (Reuters), 29 t & b (Reuters);
Topham Picturepoint pp. 3, 6 b.

Contents

1. What is NATO?

The North Atlantic Treaty Organization (NATO) was set up in 1949 by 12 countries in Europe and North America, including the United Kingdom and the United States. More European countries have joined over the years, and by 2003 NATO had 19 members and another seven set to join.

Joining forces

NATO is a political and military alliance. It was formed soon after the Second World War, when the threat of further conflict seemed very real. The NATO countries wanted to defend themselves against a possible attack by the Soviet Union (the communist state that included present-day Russia and Ukraine).

◀ *Representatives of NATO countries and other friendly states meet at NATO's headquarters in Brussels in 1995.*

▶ *NATO was formed after war had devastated Europe.*

Checklist

NATO members

Country	Year joined
Belgium	1949
Canada	1949
Czech Republic	1999
Denmark	1949
France	1949
West Germany	1955
Greece	1952
Hungary	1999
Iceland	1949
Italy	1949
Luxembourg	1949
Netherlands	1949
Norway	1949
Poland	1999
Portugal	1949
Spain	1982
Turkey	1952
United Kingdom	1949
United States	1949

To join in 2004:
Bulgaria, Estonia, Latvia, Lithuania, Romania, Slovakia and Slovenia.

The NATO member countries agreed that an attack on any one of them would be seen as an attack on them all. They formed a joint military command so that in the event of one country being attacked, all the other countries would be able to launch a co-ordinated defence of that country. Any decision of this kind would be made jointly by the governments of the NATO member countries. Although NATO was officially an alliance of equal independent states, because of the United States' huge size and strength, it has often taken the leadership role in the organization.

With time, NATO became a massively powerful military alliance. Until the early 1990s, NATO was in confrontation with the countries united under the Warsaw Pact (an alliance of East European countries led by the Soviet Union). This confrontation, which involved no actual fighting, was known as the Cold War.

▲ The NATO symbol has represented security for millions of people since 1949.

Promoting peace and democracy

NATO also has a wider purpose than that of a defensive military alliance. Its declared aims are to defend democracy and freedom, and promote peace and stability throughout the area of Europe and North America. Since the end of communist rule in Eastern Europe in the late 1980s, and the collapse of the Soviet Union in 1991, NATO countries have had no enemy state that could seriously threaten them. As a result, defence has become less important and the wider goals of promoting peace and democracy have come to the forefront of the organization's work.

In the 1990s NATO led peacekeeping operations in war-torn Bosnia and Herzegovina, and intervened in conflict in the southern Serbian province of Kosovo. Since 2000 NATO has made efforts to establish good relations with its former enemies, most notably trying to build up an atmosphere of trust and co-operation with Russia and Ukraine.

▶ Civilians in the Bosnian capital, Sarajevo, shelter from the fire of a Serbian sniper while a Bosnian soldier shoots back. NATO peacekeepers have helped stop this kind of fighting in Bosnia.

Problem

In the name of democracy

One of NATO's major problems was that it claimed to be defending freedom and democracy, but some member countries were not democracies – Greece from 1967 to 1974, and Turkey for much of that time. Since the mid-1970s, however, all NATO members have been stable democracies and most have fairly good human rights records. After the death of General Franco in 1975, Spain became a democracy, and the Spanish people voted to join NATO in a referendum in 1982.

Problem

An aggressive presence?

NATO is not a popular organization with everyone. At different times many people, especially in Europe, have been hostile to it for a variety of reasons. They have, for example, seen it as a means for the United States to dominate Europe, or as an aggressive and bullying military power. But NATO sees itself as a force for good. Its supporters say it has maintained peace, preventing any major war happening in Europe for over half a century.

The structure of NATO

NATO's headquarters are in Brussels, Belgium. About 3,000 people work there. Each member state has an ambassador at NATO headquarters, and these ambassadors meet at least once a week as the North Atlantic Council (NAC). The Council is the main decision-making body of the organization. Occasionally, the foreign ministers of the member countries or even their heads of government meet in a special session of the Council. Meetings of the Council are chaired by NATO's secretary-general, who is selected from the member countries. In 2003, Jaap de Hoop Scheffer of the Netherlands became Secretary-General of NATO, a post he will hold for four years.

▼ Flags of member states fly outside the NATO headquarters building in Brussels, Belgium. At the centre is the organization's own flag.

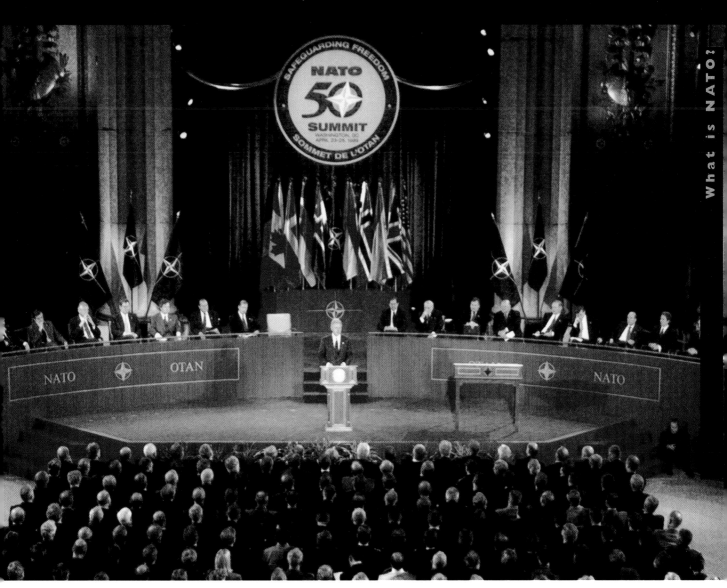

▲ In April 1999 in Washington D.C., US President Bill Clinton speaks at a ceremony celebrating the 50th anniversary of the founding of NATO.

From the outside, NATO's decision-making process looks lengthy. This is because it is based on consensus, meaning that all decisions have to be unanimous. That way, the independence of each member country is preserved and any decisions are backed by all NATO members.

The military side of NATO is headed by a Military Committee made up of chiefs of staff from each member country. NATO does not have independent armed forces. The troops and equipment available to NATO remain under the control of their own government until such time as they are needed. Then, by agreement with each government, NATO forces will set about the next task, whether that be defence, peacekeeping or in response to a natural disaster.

2. How NATO was formed

The countries that had decided to combine forces officially marked their commitment to each other's defence by signing a treaty – the North Atlantic Treaty. It was signed in the capital of the United States, Washington, D.C., on 4th April 1949 and the North Atlantic Treaty Organization – NATO – came into being. To understand the need for such an organization, it is important to consider the events that led up to its formation.

▲ US President Harry S. Truman signs the North Atlantic Treaty in 1949, committing his country to the defence of Western Europe.

▼ Soviet troops in Berlin, 1948. After the war, Germany split in two: West Germany was democratic, East Germany communist. Its capital Berlin, in East Germany, was split along similar lines.

Europe's Iron Curtain

During the Second World War, which ended in 1945, an alliance that included the Soviet Union, the United Kingdom and the United States defeated Nazi Germany. But after the war, the Soviet Union soon fell out with its former allies in the West. During the war, the Soviet army had occupied Europe as far west as central Germany. After the war, the areas under Soviet occupation, including Czechoslovakia, Hungary and Poland, were put under Soviet-style communist governments, which had little respect for human rights. Europe was now divided in two – Soviet communism in the east and liberal democracy in the west – a divide which became known as 'the Iron Curtain'.

In comparison to the Soviet forces, the armies of West European countries such as France and the United Kingdom were weak. If the Soviet Union attacked them, they would not be able to defend themselves successfully. West European leaders, such as British Foreign Secretary Ernest Bevin, thought the answer was to enlist the help of another powerful liberal democracy, the United States. They hoped the United States would commit itself to defending Western Europe against a possible Soviet attack.

▲ *Ernest Bevin (above), UK Foreign Secretary 1945-51, played a large part in the creation of NATO.*

◀ *In 1948-49, the Soviet Union tried to take over West Berlin by blockading the city. This was broken by 'the Berlin Airlift' – British and American aircraft flying in supplies from outside.*

The United States and NATO

At the end of the Second World War, the United States had withdrawn most of its forces from Europe. Traditionally there was great hostility in the United States to the idea of permanent alliances with foreign countries – Americans liked to keep out of foreigners' quarrels.

But by 1947 the United States' government, led by President Harry S. Truman, had become concerned about the possible spread of communism worldwide. The United States did not want to see Western Europe come under communist rule, either through a Soviet invasion or by some form of communist revolution anywhere in Western Europe.

In June 1947 the United States Congress passed the Marshall Plan, under which the United States provided massive economic aid for the rebuilding of Western Europe and the reinforcement of democratic government there.

It was European countries themselves who made the first moves towards a military alliance with the United States. In March 1948 the Brussels Treaty created the Western Union, a defensive alliance between Belgium, France, Luxembourg, the Netherlands and the United Kingdom. The Western Union then began negotiations to expand the alliance to include Canada and the United States, as well as other European countries. The final list of founder members of the alliance that became NATO was: Belgium, Canada, Denmark, France, Iceland, Italy, Luxembourg, the Netherlands, Norway, Portugal, the United Kingdom and the United States.

▼ *The communist threat was embodied by the Soviet dictator Josef Stalin. Here his picture dominates a 1940s shop window in communist-ruled Czechoslovakia.*

Spotlight

The terms of the Treaty

The North Atlantic Treaty of 1949, which is still in force today, starts by stating that the member governments 'desire to live in peace with all peoples and all governments'. It maintains that they are determined 'to safeguard the freedom, common heritage and civilization of their peoples, founded on the principles of democracy, individual liberty and the rule of law'. The NATO countries agree 'to promote stability and well being' and to 'unite for collective defence'.

The Treaty also states that the original members can invite any other European country to join NATO, if it seems suitable.

Shared values

All member countries were keen to stress shared heritage and common values as the main reason for the alliance. They did not want to be seen as purely a military alliance, let alone an aggressive one. But in spite of this, the formation of the alliance seemed like an act of aggression to the Soviet Union.

When the Washington Treaty founding NATO was signed, no one knew for certain how important the organization would become. The United States remained lukewarm about any real military commitment to the defence of Western Europe but this soon changed as US fears of communism increased. NATO, being an organization that united the governments of several countries, became a dominant force in international politics.

3. NATO in the Cold War

For 40 years after its creation in 1949, NATO was a key player in the armed stand-off with the Soviet Union known as the Cold War. Its military forces became the most powerful ever possessed by an alliance in the history of the world.

Soon after the NATO treaty was signed, the Soviet Union exploded its first atom bomb, China became a communist country and war broke out in Korea between the communist North and the American-backed South. These events meant that the USA was more convinced than ever of the threat posed by communism and in response, it strengthened its commitment to the NATO alliance. American troops and aircraft were stationed in Western Europe and America's nuclear weapons were committed to the defence of its European allies.

▲ *The nuclear age: top, the first hydrogen bomb is tested; above, schoolchildren in Kansas, USA, practise their survival drill for use in case of nuclear attack.*

▲ British Prime Minister
Clement Attlee meets American bomber
crews stationed in East Anglia in 1949.

As the US military presence in Europe increased, the alliance
also expanded to increase its strength. In 1952 Greece and
Turkey joined, although neither country was a well-established
democracy. West Germany joined the alliance in 1955, an
extremely controversial move. Most of the allied countries had
fought against Germany in the First and Second World Wars, and
many people found it hard to accept the Germans as allies. The
Soviet Union saw the inclusion of West Germany in NATO as a
provocative act and responded by forming the Warsaw Pact, a
military alliance with its fellow communist countries in Eastern
Europe.

▲ French President
Charles de Gaulle, who
made NATO close its
military bases and
headquarters in France.

▼ CND campaigners
protest against nuclear
weapons in the 1960s.

Nuclear weapons

NATO and the Warsaw Pact countries became involved in a
dangerous 'arms race', with each side accumulating ever more
lethal weapons of mass destruction. Rather than making the two
sides feel more secure, however, these arms only increased the
fear of war. This was especially true of nuclear weapons. By the
1960s, both the United States and the Soviet Union had
developed vast nuclear armouries, capable of destroying most of
the world's population.

NATO was committed to using nuclear weapons, if necessary, to
defeat a Soviet invasion in Europe. However, many people in
NATO countries protested against nuclear weapons, arguing that

Spotlight

De Gaulle against NATO

General Charles de Gaulle, president of France from 1958 to 1969, resented NATO because he saw it as a threat to France's independence. He insisted that France should have its own nuclear weapons, an 'independent nuclear deterrent' under French control.

Spotlight

The NATO alliance has traditionally been restricted to Europe and the North Atlantic – it does not commit its members to support one other anywhere else in the world. For instance, when the United States became involved in the Vietnam War in the 1960s, NATO countries such as the United Kingdom did not send troops to help their ally. In 2003, however, NATO took control of peacekeeping forces in Afghanistan, its first step outside the Euro-Atlantic area.

they threatened the future of humanity. The British organization, the Campaign for Nuclear Disarmament (CND), was a particularly effective anti-nuclear movement. Protests were especially intense in the 1980s when American cruise missiles with nuclear warheads were sited in Western Europe to counter the threat of Soviet warheads in Eastern Europe.

Divisions in the alliance

There were at times sharp differences among NATO members. Greece and Turkey were generally on hostile terms with one another and came close to open warfare on several occasions. More importantly, there were tensions between European countries and the United States. Many Europeans – including France's President Charles de Gaulle – viewed NATO as an organization used by the Americans to dominate Europe. Some Americans, on the other hand, said that Europeans should contribute more money to their own defence.

In 1966 de Gaulle withdrew France from the military side of NATO. All NATO bases on French soil were closed down and the organization was forced to relocate its headquarters from Paris to Brussels. Despite this, France remains committed to the defence of its allies, so in practice it has made only a small difference to its participation in the alliance.

▲ Politics forgotten, European fans were delighted when Elvis Presley served as a soldier at a NATO base in Europe.

▲ *A Royal Navy Polaris submarine, part of NATO's nuclear armoury.*

The end of the Cold War

Over the years the existence of two armed camps – NATO on one side and the Warsaw Pact countries on the other – became an accepted part of international politics. By the late 1960s, few people seriously expected the Soviet Union to invade Western Europe. Moves were made to reduce tensions and the risk of nuclear war. But this 'detente', or relaxing of attitudes, failed to solve the fundamental problem of a divided Europe, and nuclear arsenals continued to grow. Then, in 1985, Mikhail Gorbachev became ruler of the Soviet Union.

▲ *The Berlin Wall divided East Berlin from West Berlin from 1961 to 1989.*

Gorbachev wanted to reform the communist system and end the Cold War. In 1987 he reached a landmark agreement with US President Ronald Reagan to reduce nuclear weapons. Over the next two years, communist rule in Eastern Europe literally fell apart, culminating in the dramatic breaking down of the Berlin Wall, which had divided communist East Berlin from democratic West Berlin for 28 years. Two years later, at the end of 1991, communist rule ended in the Soviet Union itself. The Soviet Union broke up, being replaced by an independent Russia, Ukraine and 15 other states.

▶ *US President Ronald Reagan and Soviet leader Mikhail Gorbachev (left) agreed to cuts in nuclear arsenals.*

NATO appeared to have fulfilled its primary objective but it soon became clear that although the type of threats to peace had changed, the need for security and peace had not gone away.

NATO was originally formed to resist the threat of war posed by the Soviet Union. By the end of 1991, the Soviet Union no longer existed. The communist Warsaw Pact was disbanded, but NATO did not break up. Instead more countries than ever were clamouring to join the organization.

Until the 1990s, NATO's focus had been on mutual defence – the part of the treaty that stated that all the allies would come to the aid of any member country that was under attack. After the end of communist rule in Eastern Europe and the break-up of the Soviet Union, however, there was no enemy state that could realistically attack the NATO allies.

At the same time, though, Europe became less stable. Wars broke out in Yugoslavia and the territories of the former Soviet Union. Throughout the areas once under communist rule, new governments faced severe political and economic problems.

▼ Social and economic conditions in post-communist Russia were very difficult: below, a beggar sleeps in a Moscow street; bottom, poor people pick over garbage in a rubbish tip.

▲ *Former NATO Secretary-General Lord Robertson (right) welcoming a representative of Croatia into the Partnership for Peace – a major NATO initiative in the post-Cold War era.*

NATO's focus shifted from mutual defence to other parts of the original treaty, which said that member states would promote 'conditions of stability and well-being', preserve 'peace and security', and strengthen democratic government. NATO decided that its major role would be to encourage peace, security and stability throughout Europe, especially in the large areas previously under communist rule.

Partnership for Peace

In 1994 NATO asked European countries outside the alliance to join a 'Partnership for Peace'. Today, almost all non-NATO countries in Europe have joined the Partnership. Members include Russia, Ukraine and the other states that had made up the Soviet Union; the other former members of the Warsaw Pact; and previously neutral countries such as Austria, Finland, Ireland, Sweden and Switzerland.

Checklist

Partnership for Peace

In 2000, 26 non-NATO countries were part of the Partnership for Peace. They were:

Albania	Kazakhstan
Armenia	Kyrghyz
Austria	Republic
Azerbaijan	Latvia
Belarus	Lithuania
Bulgaria	Moldova
Croatia	Romania
Estonia	Russia
Finland	Slovakia
Former	Slovenia
Yugoslav	Sweden
Republic of	Switzerland
Macedonia	Turkmenistan
(FYROM)	Ukraine
Georgia	Uzbekistan
Ireland	

Although the Soviet Union and its communist allies no longer exist, their armies and weapons are still there – including nuclear weapons. These armies were trained to fight against NATO and to defend communism. Through the Partnership for Peace NATO hoped to break down the barriers between itself and its former enemies, and ensure that these once communist armed forces would adapt to democracy.

The Partnership has mainly encouraged co-operation among the armed forces of the countries involved, especially arranging joint training exercises. The focus has been on preparing for peacekeeping missions and for helping to cope with natural or man-made disasters.

▼ *An American sergeant shows an Estonian soldier how to defuse a landmine during a Partnership for Peace military exercise.*

▲ *American and Russian soldiers co-operate in the peacekeeping Stabilization Force in Bosnia.*

Turning enemies into allies

As part of its new initiative for peace, NATO decided to start inviting former Warsaw Pact countries to become full members of the alliance – a step that was not popular with all its members. In 1997, three countries – the Czech Republic, Hungary and Poland – were invited to join NATO. This selection was based on the view that they had become sufficiently similar to the countries of the West – that is, they had stable democratic governments and modernizing economies. After two years of negotiations, the three countries joined NATO.

Links with Russia and Ukraine, the largest countries of the former Soviet Union, were much harder to develop. Both still had nuclear weapons and, especially in Russia, an active suspicion of NATO. The alliance made great efforts to convince the Russians of its goodwill. In 1997 a NATO-Russia Permanent Joint Council was set up to provide a formal structure for building trust and co-operation between NATO countries and Russia.

Spotlight

Peacekeeping in Bosnia

NATO's new peacekeeping role in Europe has been demonstrated in Bosnia. A war that had broken out when Bosnia was trying to gain independence from Yugoslavia in 1992 was ended by a peace agreement in 1995. NATO sent an Implementation Force (IFOR) into Bosnia to prevent further fighting and help create stability so that peace could be achieved and democracy could begin to take root. Other countries joined in the effort, including Russia and non-NATO members of the Partnership for Peace. In 2004, many of these troops were still in Bosnia as a Stabilization Force (SFOR), committed to preserving the peace, helping displaced people return home and seeking out war criminals.

▼ *US Secretary of State Madeleine Albright looks on as the Czech Republic, Hungary and Poland sign up for NATO in 1999.*

The Mediterranean Dialogue

In 1994 NATO launched the 'Mediterranean Dialogue', which set up regular discussions between the alliance and states in North Africa and the eastern Mediterranean, including Algeria, Egypt, Israel, Jordan, Morocco and Tunisia. The aim was to encourage peace and stability throughout the Mediterranean region as instability in these areas could easily spill over into the NATO countries.

Growing pains

The expansion of NATO to include the Czech Republic, Hungary and Poland in 1999 raised problems for the organization. At the start of the 1990s, the armies in the three new member states consisted of poorly paid and demoralised troops equipped with old Soviet weapons. Few of them spoke English or French, the two official languages of the alliance. This situation was soon much improved. NATO had to adapt to help the new country members, but enjoyed the benefits of the extra security their inclusion brought.

▼ *Representatives of NATO and non-NATO countries meet at the NATO headquarters in Brussels for regular talks about matters of general concern.*

Russia was wary of any expansion of NATO eastward, seeing it as a threat to its own security. To calm Russian fears, NATO agreed that no foreign troops or nuclear weapons would be stationed on the territory of the new allies. Instead NATO would use a rapid reaction force to defend the new members if they were ever attacked.

5. NATO in Kosovo

In 1999, 50 years after it was founded, NATO fought a war, attacking Serbia from the air with missiles and bombs. The move was provoked by what was happening in the province of Kosovo: namely large-scale violation of human rights and vast numbers of people being forced to leave their homes. There were also fears that the troubles and unrest would spread throughout the region. The resulting conflict was highly controversial.

▼ *Former Serbian president Slobodan Milosevic greeting his supporters. He led Serbia into conflict with NATO over Kosovo in 1999.*

The Kosovo war stemmed from the break-up of the communist state of Yugoslavia in the early 1990s. Bosnia and Herzegovina, Croatia, Macedonia and Slovenia declared themselves independent countries. Yugoslavia continued to exist, made up of two republics, Montenegro and Serbia.

Led by President Slobodan Milosevic, the Serbs opposed the independence of the former Yugoslav republics, especially Bosnia. The war in Bosnia between Croats, Muslims and Serbs, saw tens of thousands of people die, many killed in cold blood during 'ethnic cleansing' operations. The United Nations originally led the international efforts to halt the terrible fighting and NATO became involved in support of their work.

The path to war

In 1998 the focus of the war in former Yugoslavia shifted to Kosovo, a province of Serbia where the majority of the population were Albanians and the minority were Serbs. The Kosovo Liberation Army (KLA), an Albanian guerrilla movement, was fighting for independence from Serb rule. Faced with evidence of mass killings of Kosovars by Serb forces and of thousands more being driven from their homes, NATO leaders threatened Serbia with air attacks. The Serbs backed down, and agreed to take part in peace talks with the KLA, organized by NATO member states.

Difficult peace negotiations went on until March 1999. NATO repeatedly used the threat of air attacks in an attempt to make Serbia accept the presence of a NATO-led peace force in Kosovo. When it became obvious that Serbia would not accept NATO's peace initiatives, and the number of Kosovar Albanians being forced from their homes had reached more than 250,000, the NATO leaders carried out their threat. NATO air attacks began on 24 March 1999. Serbia responded by launching an offensive against the Kosovar Albanians. About half a million Kosovars fled from their homes to refugee camps in neighbouring countries.

▲ The then British Minister of Defence, George Robertson, favoured NATO action in Kosovo.

◀ Kosovar refugees driven from their homes by Serb forces.

While evidence kept coming out from Kosovo about massacres being carried out by the Serbs, NATO bombs and missiles also killed about 500 civilians, including Kosovar Albanians whom NATO was intending to help. In one incident, NATO mistakenly destroyed the Chinese Embassy in the Serb capital, Belgrade, causing a diplomatic storm.

Arriving at a peace settlement

NATO's involvement in the Kosovo conflict led to tension between NATO and Russia since the Russians have traditional links with the Serbs. But a peace deal was finally agreed through an independent initiative – a joint approach to Serbia by Russia and the European Union. In June 1999 Serbia agreed to withdraw its forces from Kosovo, grant the province self-government, let refugees return to their homes, and allow a peacekeeping force to occupy Kosovo.

▼ *British troops are welcomed as liberators in Kosovo.*

▶ *The Chinese Embassy in Belgrade, hit by a NATO airstrike.*

While NATO leaders described the war as a success, their task was not finished. The United Nations asked NATO to deploy a peacekeeping force, including Russian troops, to uphold the peace settlement and create stability in the area. This force, known as KFOR (Kosovo Force), was faced with huge problems. It had to try to restore security and order for both the Albanian and Serb people of the area, and help rebuild the province. The scale of this task put considerable strain on its staff and resources.

▶ *British Prime Minister Tony Blair saw the Kosovo war as a battle for human rights.*

▼ *A protest in Belgrade against NATO's air strikes on Serbia.*

Criticism of NATO's role in Kosovo

NATO leaders described the Kosovo war as being motivated largely by a desire to uphold human rights. It was their duty to intervene to protect the Kosovars from Serb violence and oppression. British Prime Minister Tony Blair said during the war: 'We are fighting not for territory but for values, for a new internationalism where the brutal repression of whole ethnic groups will no longer be tolerated.'

But some critics of the war saw it as an act of aggression, the bullying of a small nation – Serbia – by the major powers with their immensely powerful weaponry. NATO leaders certainly disliked the Serbian leader Slobodan Milosevic, and were glad when he lost power in October 2000, a downfall to which the war had contributed.

When NATO intervened in Kosovo, it did not have the approval of the UN Security Council. This has caused some people to say that although it could be called 'legitimate', it was in fact an illegal action.

◀ *This passenger train was hit by a NATO missile, killing or injuring dozens of civilians.*

Several times during the Kosovo war NATO aircraft struck civilian targets, including bridges, a television station and convoys of Kosovar refugees. Criticising NATO, Human Rights Watch says that some of these were not appropriate military targets under international law. As a result, unnecessarily large numbers of civilians were killed – probably 500 in all. Whilst some bombs were accidents, others did hit their intended targets.

Human Rights Watch also feel that KFOR, led by NATO, were not sufficiently experienced in law enforcement to achieve a feeling of security for people after the war. As a result, most Serbian people left Kosovo, even though the peacekeepers were on the streets, thus causing another tragedy in the form of more refugees.

▲ *The headquarters of Milosevic's Socialist Party in Belgrade burns after a NATO air attack.*

6. The future for NATO

At the end of the Cold War, many people questioned NATO's relevance. But events such as the 11 September 2001 terrorist attacks in the United States and the subsequent wars in Afghanistan and Iraq demonstrate how unstable the world still is.

Since the 11 September attacks, NATO has played a leading part in efforts to stop terrorism. It has developed plans to deal with a possible terrorist act involving chemical, nuclear or biological weapons, while maintaining its peacekeeping role in the Balkans and, from 2003, in Afghanistan.

▼ *British troops serve with the Stabilization Force in Bosnia. This kind of peacekeeping operation is one of the major justifications for the continued existence of NATO.*

For some NATO leaders, among them British Prime Minister Tony Blair, the Kosovo war seemed to point to a new mission for NATO as the upholder of human rights in Europe. But not all NATO states were keen on the idea of further military intervention in trouble spots. Some argued that the use of force caused more problems than it solved – increasing instability and making a permanent peace harder to establish.

▼ Bosnian, Croatian and Serbian leaders met to agree an end to the Bosnian conflict in 1995. But the situation in the Yugoslav region remained unsettled.

The EU and NATO

Because of its military might, the United States has supplied much of the weaponry and armed forces when NATO has intervened in a crisis. However, the European NATO members' dependence on the United States is an ongoing issue, as it has been since the founding of the organization. As ties between European Union (EU) countries – most are also NATO members – became closer during the late 1990s, discussions centred around the creation of a European Rapid Reaction Force. This would be a multi-national force that could deal with crisis spots without the aid of the United States.

However, most member states have very little in the way of military resources compared with the United States. Therefore, at present, the proposed force would not be able to form a 'Euro-Army' nor an alternative to NATO. It would merely use NATO resources for its own operations in cases where the United States did not want to get involved.

Expanding alliance

The NATO alliance continued to expand in the new millennium. The integration of Hungary, Poland and the Czech Republic into the alliance was followed in 2002 by an invitation for seven more former communist countries to join (see page 4). Talks aimed at bringing these countries into the alliance in 2004 made rapid progress.

Fears that expansion of NATO would harm relations with Russia and Ukraine seemed to have proved unfounded. Instead, there were ever closer contacts between those countries and NATO. In 2002 the NATO-Russia Council was set up, providing regular meetings between Russia and NATO members. A NATO-Ukraine Commission fulfilled a similar function. The NATO countries were very keen to have Russia and Ukraine on their side in the war against terrorism.

▶ *Vladimir Putin, who became Russian President in 2000, has helped to improve relations between Russia and NATO.*

● Spotlight

The Chechnya crisis

In the winter of 1999–2000, Russia crushed an independence movement in the republic of Chechnya, a part of the Russian Federation. Russia's conduct was widely criticised, with well-substantiated allegations of massacres and other atrocities committed by Russian forces. Yet, unlike in Kosovo, NATO did not intervene to stop the massacres, nor did it even put extreme pressure on Russia to change its behaviour.

The events in Chechnya (see panel) brought a clash between NATO's commitment to upholding human rights and its need to work with Russia. The NATO countries could not hope to win Russian support for the war against terrorism if they opposed Russia over the way it dealt with Chechnya.

▶ *Russian soldiers in action in Chechnya.*

▼ *Russia used tanks against lightly armed Chechen fighters.*

The future of NATO

Today, NATO's work is based on the view that peace is best maintained by creating forums for discussion and through cooperation between nations. Between them, the NATO countries still maintain a substantial stock of nuclear and non-nuclear weapons, but the alliance's modern roles mostly require smaller, flexible mobile forces rather than the huge military might of the past. The future of the alliance depends on the continuing support of the people of Europe and North America for the idea that NATO is essential to guarantee security.

Spotlight

Disaster relief

NATO is increasingly involved in disaster relief. In 1999 NATO opened a Euro-Atlantic Disaster Relief Co-ordination Centre to enable it to co-ordinate emergency and relief operations in the event of a disaster, man-made or natural. Examples of natural disasters that have led NATO forces to respond to calls for help are floods in Ukraine in 1999 and forest fires in Portugal in 2003.

▲ Victims of the Ukraine floods in 1999. NATO troops helped in the relief of this natural disaster.

▼ The fall of the Berlin Wall in 1989: a victory for democracy – and for NATO?

Spotlight

In 1997, proposing that his country should join NATO, the Polish Foreign Minister, Bronislav Geremek, made a powerful case for the continued existence of the alliance. He said:

'We would prefer to live in a Europe with no arms and no alliances. But we do live in a world where military power remains the ultimate guarantor of security. NATO is an alliance which has managed to put its immense military might in service of fundamental values and principles that we share. NATO can make Europe safe for democracy. No other organization can replace the alliance in this role.'

Glossary

arms race   situation that arises when two or more countries or alliances constantly try to have more powerful arms than the other, leading to the development of even more powerful weapons in even larger numbers

atrocities   extremely cruel, brutal acts, especially against defenceless people

Cold War   the armed confrontation between the United States and its allies on one side and the communist Soviet Union and its allies on the other, which lasted from the late 1940s to the 1980s

communism   political and economic system whereby everyone works for the common good rather than individual gain. As the government is not elected democratically, it is almost impossible for the people to remove bad government.

democracy   political system in which the people elect their rulers

detente   reducing tensions that might lead to war

dictatorship   rule by an individual who has more or less absolute power over his or her country

ethnic cleansing   driving all people of a particular ethnic group out of the place where they live by force or terror

guerrillas   lightly armed fighters usually engaged in a war against the government of their own country

heritage   traditions and values handed down from the past

human rights   freedoms that all humans should have the right to enjoy, wherever they live and whatever their government

Iron Curtain   a phrase coined by British statesman Winston Churchill to describe the fortified line that divided Western Europe from communist-ruled Eastern Europe from the late 1940s to the 1980s

military alliance   an agreement between countries to fight together against a common enemy

Useful information

neutral — not taking sides in a conflict or confrontation

nuclear weapons — weapons of immense destructive power using the energy from the nuclei in atoms

referendum — a vote taken amongst a country's population on a specific issue

self-government — the right of the people of a particular area within a country to choose their own government but not have full independence from that country

Soviet Union — the communist state which until 1991 ruled a vast area of Europe and Asia, including Russia, Ukraine, Belarus, Georgia, Armenia and Kazakhstan

terrorist — a member of a political movement that uses violence to achieve its goals

Warsaw Pact — military alliance set up in 1955 by the Soviet Union and the communist countries of Eastern Europe

NATO Headquarters
Boulevard Leopold III
1110 Brussels
Belgium

NATO website:
www.nato.int
This site provides a brief history of the organization, regularly updated information on current topics such as Kosovo, details of NATO's policy agreements and access to an extensive archive of documentary material.

Human Rights Watch
2nd Floor, 2–12 Pentonville Road
London
N1 9HF

Human Rights Watch website:
www.hrw.org
This site provides a mass of research on human rights issues around the world.

Amnesty International
99-119 Rosebery Avenue
London
EC1R 4RE

Amnesty International website:
www.amnesty.org.uk
Deals with human rights issues generally.

Index